How Did We
Find Out About
Blood?

The "HOW DID WE FIND OUT . . .?" SERIES
by Isaac Asimov

HOW DID WE FIND OUT—
The Earth Is Round?
About Electricity?
About Numbers?
About Dinosaurs?
About Germs?
About Vitamins?
About Comets?
About Energy?
About Atoms?
About Nuclear Power?
About Outer Space?
About Earthquakes?
About Black Holes?
About Our Human Roots?
About Antarctica?
About Oil?
About Coal?
About Solar Power?
About Volcanoes?
About Life in the Deep Sea?
About the Beginning of Life?
About the Universe?
About Genes?
About Computers?
About Robots?
About the Atmosphere?
About DNA?
About the Speed of Light?
About Blood?

How Did We
Find Out About
Blood?

Isaac Asimov

Illustrated by David Wool

Walker and Company
New York

First published in the United States of America
in 1986 by the Walker Publishing Company, Inc.

Published simultaneously in Canada by John Wiley & Sons
Canada, Limited, Rexdale, Ontario.

Library of Congress Cataloging-in-Publication Data

Asimov, Isaac, 1920-
How did we find out about blood?

(The "How did we find out—?" series)
Includes index.
Summary: Traces the development of scientific
knowledge about the functions of blood in the body,
from beliefs held by the ancient Greeks to discoveries
in more modern times.
1. Blood—Circulation—Research—History—Juvenile
literature. [1. Blood] I. Wool, David, ill.
II. Title. III. Series: Asimov, Isaac, 1920-
How did we find out—series.
QP103.A85   1986   612'.1'09   86-15844
ISBN 0-8027-6647-1

ISBN 0-8027-6649-8 (lib. bdg.)

Printed in the United States of America

10 9 8 7 6 5 4 3 2 1

To Jocelyn Wilkes and Priscilla Reeves
together again in Ruddygore

Contents

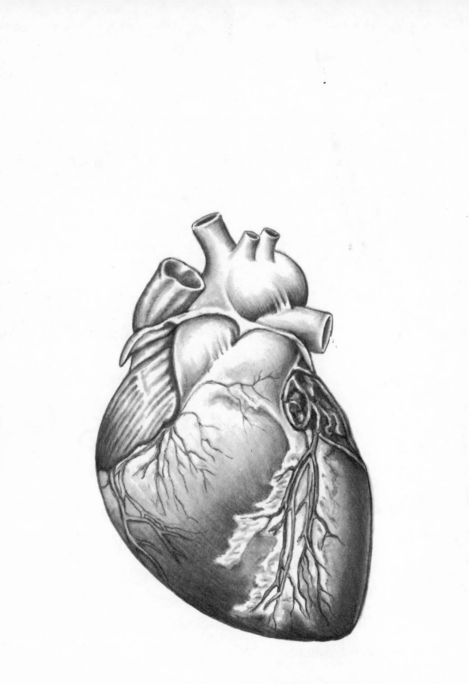

The heart

1

The Heart

IF WE CUT ourselves, we bleed. Animals bleed, too, when they are cut. So we know that blood exists.

We quickly find out that it's important, too. People who lose a lot of blood grow very weak as a result. It takes them time to become well again. If they lose too much blood, they die.

Because of this, some people once thought that blood actually *was* life, that it was the living part of the body.

In the Bible, for instance, the Israelites are told they must not eat meat with blood in it. In the Book of Deuteronomy (chapter 12, verse 23) it says: "Only be sure that thou eat not the blood: for the blood is the life."

That can't be right, however, for people and animals can die, even when they don't lose any blood at all. That doesn't mean that blood isn't important to life. It just means that blood isn't the only thing that's important.

About 400 B.C., the ancient Greek doctor Hippocrates (hih-POK-ruh-teez, 460–370 B.C.) and his followers thought there were four important fluids in the body, one of them blood. Health, they said, depended on the proper balance among the four fluids.

Nowadays, we know the matter of health is far more complicated than that, but we've never stopped thinking that blood is an extremely important part of it.

Blood doesn't just lie motionless in the body. Sometimes, when a person is badly cut, the blood seems to spurt out. What's more, the spurting seems to be in time with the beating of the heart, so people got the notion that the heart must squeeze and push blood out of itself, over and over again.

Everyone's heart beats. You can feel your own heartbeat if you place your hand on your chest. It beats regularly, about seventy times a minute in grown-ups; a little faster in children. The heart beats as long as you live, and when it stops, you die.

That makes it look as though it's not just blood that's important to life, but *moving* blood, and therefore the heart.

In fact, some ancients thought that the heart was the living and feeling part of the body. After all, your heart beats faster and harder if you are frightened or very angry, so perhaps it controls the emotions. It also speeds up when you run around or work hard, and it slows down when you're asleep. When you're more active, it's more active, and when you're less active, it's less active.

The Greek philosopher Aristotle (AR-is-tot-l, 384–322 B.C.) was so impressed by the importance of the heart, that he thought it might be the part of the body that does the thinking. He was wrong there, but the heart is very important just the same.

How can you tell what's going on inside the body? You can't just cut open a living body and look inside. You would cause great pain and kill a human being if you did that. You might cut open and look into a dead body, but most people in ancient times thought even that was a terrible thing to do and usually such a "dissection" (dis-SEK-shun), from Latin words meaning "to cut apart," was not allowed.

Of course, animals were cut open, either because they were being prepared for cooking, or being used as a sacrifice to the gods.

Butchers weren't interested in studying the parts of the animals. They were just preparing cuts of meat for sale or for cooking.

Priests who sacrificed animals were sometimes interested in some of the internal parts, because they thought the shapes of those parts could give them hints for foretelling the future. (That was quite wrong, of course.) Fortune-telling didn't take long, and they didn't study the animal carefully. And even if they did, animal parts are sometimes different from human parts in important ways.

It was not until after Aristotle's time that scientists began to study the inside of the human body carefully.

In the city of Alexandria, Egypt, a place of study and learning was established. It was called the Museum, and in it, between 300 and 250 B.C., there was careful dissection of dead human bodies. The structure of the body was studied. This is called "anatomy" (uh-NAT-tuh-mee), from Greek words meaning "to cut up."

About 300 B.C., a Greek physician, Praxagoras (prak-SAG-uh-ras) showed that there were tubes connected to the heart. Some of these were filled with blood. We call them "veins" (VANEZ).

Another kind of tube, also connected to the heart, was empty and contained only air. Praxagoras thought they carried air to different parts of the body. We still call those tubes "arteries" (AHR-tuh-reez), from Greek words meaning "air-carrier." Arteries and veins are called blood vessels.

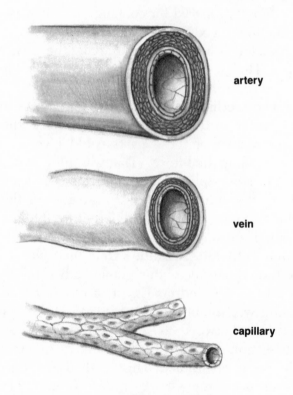

artery

vein

capillary

Blood vessels

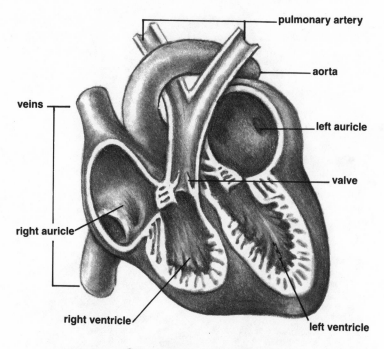

pulmonary artery

aorta

veins

left auricle

valve

right auricle

right ventricle

left ventricle

Cross section of heart

From dissection studies, doctors knew where the arteries were to be found in living bodies. Praxagoras's student, Herophilus found that where the arteries came near the skin, you could feel a beating, just as though it were a little heart. This is called a "pulse." He thought that the arteries carried blood as the veins did, and did not carry air.

That is so. The heart spurts blood into the arteries. With each beat of the heart, the thick, muscular wall of the artery expands as blood is forced through, and then the wall contracts again. It is this that causes the pulse. The veins, with thinner, less muscular walls, carry blood quietly.

Galen c.130–c.200

As a person dies, the last heartbeat sends blood through and out of the arteries, and nothing follows. That is why dead arteries are empty. Doctors might have learned more, but the study of anatomy in Alexandria quickly stopped. Dissection was considered against the law and, for a thousand years, little more was learned.

Still, doctors knew there were arteries and veins. Why were there *two* kinds?

A Greek doctor, Galen (GAY-len, A.D. 130–200), felt that the arteries originated in the heart. The heart pumped blood into the arteries, which carried the blood to all parts of the body where it was used for nourishment. The veins, he thought, originated in the liver. There, he believed, blood was formed and was carried by the veins to the heart.

In Alexandria, though, doctors had dissected the heart. They had found it consisted of two parts, a left ventricle (VENT-rih-kul) and a right ventricle. These had thick, muscular walls, especially the left one. On top of each ventricle was a thin-walled chamber, the left atrium on one side, and the right atrium on the other. There was an opening connecting each atrium with the ventricle beneath, but there was no opening from one atrium-ventricle to the other.

It was as though the heart were actually a double pump. Each half was attached to its own arteries and veins.

But why should the heart be double? Surely a single pump would be enough.

Galen thought it *was* a single pump. He thought there might be tiny passages, or pores, through the thick, muscular wall between the two ventricles. These pores were so fine and narrow they were invisible to the eye. (This was quite wrong, but people continued to believe it for about fourteen hundred years after Galen.)

About 1300, doctors in Italy began to dissect dead bodies again. In 1316, an Italian doctor, Mondino de Luzzi (mon-DEE-noh day LOOTS-tsee, 1275–1326), wrote the first book that dealt entirely with anatomy. It contained mostly what Galen had taught, however.

But then, in 1543, a Belgian anatomist, Andreas Vesalius (veh-SAY-lee-us, 1514–1564), made his own studies and published a far better anatomy book. The art of printing had now been developed, and Vesalius's book was in type and had beautiful illustrations. It was read throughout Europe, and it started scientists on a whole new track where the human body was concerned.

However, Vesalius couldn't improve on Galen's theories as far as the workings of the heart were concerned.

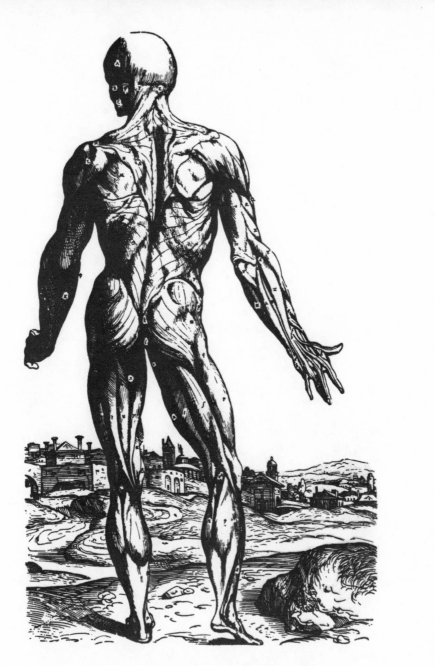

Anatomical drawing by Vesalius, 1543

2
The
Circulation

ALTHOUGH THE EUROPEAN doctors didn't know it,
Galen *had* been improved on. It happened in the
East, and the man who did it was a Syrian doctor, Ibn
al-Nafis (is-n-al-NA-fis, 1210–1288).

In 1242, he wrote a book on surgery. In it he said
that the pores, which Galen had said allowed blood to
pass from one ventricle to the other, simply didn't
exist. The wall between the two ventricles was solid
and muscular, and nothing could leak through.

Did that mean the heart was a double pump with no
interconnection at all?

No. Ibn al-Nafis suggested another way in which
blood might go from the right ventricle to the left.

He said that when the heart contracted, the blood in the right ventricle entered the large "pulmonary artery" (PUL-muh-neh-ree). This is from the Latin word for "lung," because this artery carries blood to the lungs.

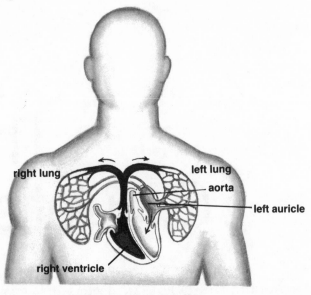

The lesser circulation

As the pulmonary artery reaches the lungs, it divides into smaller and smaller branches, as does a tree. The arterial branches get so small you can't see them without a microscope. The blood in these tiny vessels that line the lungs collects air. The tiny vessels then join into fewer and larger vessels, which are large enough to be seen again. They are veins. These become still fewer and larger until all the blood is collected into one large vessel, the "pulmonary vein."

The pulmonary vein leads the blood, now mixed with air, into the *left* atrium, from which it passes into the *left* ventricle. When the heart contracts, the blood in the left ventricle, with its air mixture, goes into the "aorta" (ay-AWR-tuh), the largest artery in the body and then moves on to all parts of the body.

Now we see why we need a double pump. It may be that the blood is formed in the liver, goes to the heart, and then travels to the rest of the body. However, it goes to the right atrium and ventricle first, is sent to the lung and back, and *then* goes to the left atrium and ventricle and to the rest of the body. The right half of the heart is needed as a special pump designed to supply the blood with air.

If we picture the blood going from the right ventricle to the lungs and then back to the heart, we say that it "circulates" (SUR-kyoo-lates), which is from Latin words meaning "to move in a circle." Actually, the trip to the lungs and back is called the "lesser circulation," because the left ventricle sends the blood on a longer journey. Ibn al-Nafis, however, had nothing to say about what happened to the blood that left the left ventricle. Presumably, it was simply used up by the body so that new blood had to be formed.

Of course, no one then could see the fine vessels in the lungs that connected the tiniest arteries with the tiniest veins, any more than they could see Galen's "pores" between the ventricles. That was a flaw in Ibn al-Nafis's suggestion.

There was another catch. No one in Europe knew about Ibn al-Nafis's book. It was not discovered until 1924, so Europeans had to make the discovery of the lesser circulation on their own. That discovery was accomplished first by the Spanish doctor, Michael Servetus (ser-VEE-tus, 1511–1553).

Servetus lived in unsettled times. The Catholic church in Western Europe had split in two. Those that broke away called themselves Protestants, and there was great hostility between the Protestants and Catholics.

Servetus managed to develop religious views that offended both the Catholics and the Protestants. In 1553, he published a book in which he expressed his views. He carefully didn't put his name on the book, but he had discussed his views so openly that everyone knew he must have written it.

In France, the Catholics arrested him, but he escaped and went to Geneva, in Switzerland. Geneva was ruled by a very strict Protestant named John Calvin (1509–1564). Calvin was so shocked by Servetus's religious views that he had him arrested and burned at the stake. He then collected all the copies he could find of Servetus's book and burned them, also.

Fortunately, a few copies survived and in 1694, a century and a half after Servetus's death, one turned up. Doctors were amazed to discover that the book not only contained his views on religion, but also described the lesser circulation of the blood to the lungs and back. By then, though, the discovery had been made a third time.

In 1559, six years after Servetus's death, an Italian doctor, Realdo Colombo (koh-LUM-boh, 1516–1559), also thought of the lesser circulation and published a book about it.

That book survived; other doctors read it, and more and more of them were convinced that Colombo was right. Even though Colombo had his idea after Servetus and *long* after Ibn al-Nafis, it was Colombo's work that European doctors knew about. It was on the basis of his work that they went on to make further discoveries. That is why Colombo gets the credit for discovering the lesser circulation.

In 1574, an Italian doctor, Girolamo Fabrici (fab-REE-chee, 1537–1619), was studying the veins in the leg. He noticed that they had little valves in them. If the blood moved in one direction, the valves folded in toward the walls of the vessel, so that the blood could pass without trouble. If the blood moved in the opposite direction, the valves opened and closed off the vein.

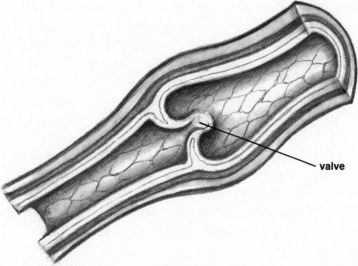

valve

Valve in a vein

This meant they were one-way valves. They permitted the blood to move when a person is standing upright. The blood can't move downward.

This makes sense. When a person moves his legs, or just tightens his leg muscles, those muscles squeeze against the veins and force the blood in those veins to move upward against the pull of gravity (because that's the only way they'll go). If a person keeps his leg muscles relaxed, the blood isn't moving much, but at least it isn't being pulled down by gravity. The valves won't allow that.

The important thing was that the blood in the leg veins could only move *toward the heart*. Fabrici paid no attention because everyone thought that the blood leaving the left ventricle always moved away from the heart. He missed the importance of his own discovery.

But then came William Harvey (1578–1657), an Englishman who, after he became a doctor, went to Italy for further education and studied under Fabrici.

Harvey dissected the hearts of dead people and studied the valves between each atrium and its ventricle. He noticed that they were one-way valves. They allowed the blood to flow from the atrium to the ventricle without any trouble. When the heart contracted, however, none of the blood in the ventricle could flow back into the atrium. Instead, all the blood was pushed out into the arteries.

Harvey began thinking about the valves his teacher, Fabrici, had discovered in the leg veins. They were one-way, and they forced the blood to move toward the heart.

He checked that by tying off and blocking different veins in animals he experimented on. The veins always bulged on the side of the block away from the heart. It was as though the blood were trying to flow toward the heart and to accumulate just below the block because it simply couldn't flow away from the heart. This was true of all veins.

William Harvey, 1578–1657

In the arteries, the blood bulged on the heart side of any block he put in, as though it were trying to flow away from the heart and couldn't move in the other direction.

Harvey now saw what was happening. The heart pushed blood into the arteries, and the blood returned by way of the veins. It did this for *both* ventricles. The blood had a *double* circulation. If one started from the right ventricle, it left by way of the arteries to the lungs, and returned by way of the veins to the left atrium and from there into the left ventricle. From the left ventricle, it left by way of the arteries to the rest of the body and returned (in a "greater circulation") by way of the veins to the right atrium and from there into the right ventricle. Then it started all over.

Harvey also showed that it was impossible to suppose that the blood was used up in the body and that new blood was formed. He measured how much blood the heart pumped in one contraction and counted the number of contractions. He found that in one hour, the heart pumped out a quantity of blood that was three times the weight of a man. The body couldn't use up blood and form new blood at such a rate. *The same blood had to circulate and be used over and over again.*

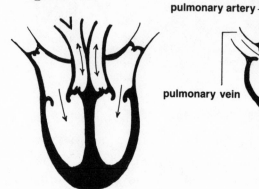

ventricle expanded   ventricle contracted

How the heart pumps

Harvey still had the same problem Ibn al-Nafis had had. The smallest arteries and veins that could be seen had to be connected by vessels too small to see. Were they really there?

In the 1650s, scientists had learned to put lenses together in such a way that objects too small to see

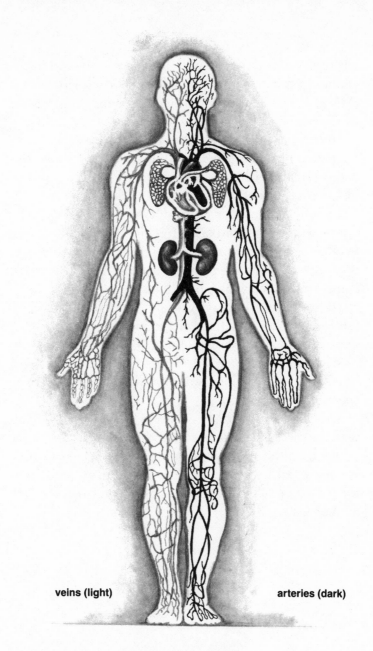

veins (light)   arteries (dark)

The circulatory system

with the naked eye could be magnified and made visible. Such instruments were called "microscopes" (MY-kroh-scopes), from Greek words meaning "to see the small."

One of the first scientists to use a microscope was an Italian named Marcello Malpighi (mal-PEE-gee, 1628–1694). With the microscope, he could see tiny blood vessels that were invisible without one.

In 1661, four years after Harvey's death, Malpighi studied the wings of bats. He could see blood vessels in their thin membranes and, under the microscope, he could see that the smallest arteries and veins were connected by very fine blood vessels.

He called these blood vessels "capillaries" (CAP-ih-leh-reez), from a Latin word for "hair," because they were as thin as the finest of hairs.

With the discovery of capillaries, the idea of the circulation of the blood was complete, and it has been accepted ever since.

An English scientist, Stephen Hales (1677–1761), was the first to measure "blood pressure," the force with which the blood is pushed along in its circulation. He reported his work in 1733. Blood pressure is now measured very frequently. "High blood pressure" is a dangerous condition.

3
The Red Cells

To THE EYE, blood looks like a red fluid, and every bit of it looks the same. Under the microscope, however, it contains little objects that float in a clear liquid. It is the little objects that give the blood its redness. The liquid is faint yellow in color, and so is one of the little objects taken by itself. However, a combination of many of the objects has a deep red color.

In the early days of the microscope these little objects were seen. Malpighi saw them. A Dutch scientist, Jan Swammerdam (SVAHM-er-dahm, 1637–1680), described them in 1658. It isn't certain which one of these two men should get the credit for being the first to see them.

Because of their color, these little objects came to be called "red cells." The word "cell" is given to the tiny units, too small to be seen except under a microscope, that build up all living things. Another name for the red cells is "erythrocytes" (ee-RITH-roh-sites), but that is just a Greek word that means "red cells."

The red cells were first studied carefully by the Dutch scientist, Anton van Leeuwenhoek (LAY-venhook, 1632–1723). He had the best of all the very early microscopes. He polished tiny lenses of clear glass into perfect curves. Looking through his lenses, he could see small objects magnified by an unusually large amount, and he could see them more clearly than anyone else could in his time.

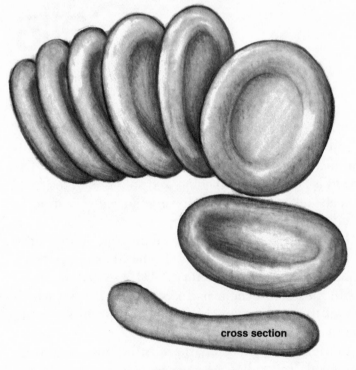

cross section

Red blood cells

Leeuwenhoek described the shape of the red cells. They are flat discs with depressions in the center. They look like tiny candy Lifesavers, but the hole in the center is not quite bored through.

Leeuwenhoek also tried to calculate their size. They are very small, smaller than most cells. It would take about 3,400 of them placed side by side to stretch across the distance of an inch. Or, if you stacked them one on top of another, it would take about 12,000 of them to make a stack an inch high.

Of course there are very many of them. Suppose you had a little square container, only 1/25 of an inch on each side and 1/25 of an inch high. Such a container would be so small you would barely be able to see it.

Imagine such a container full of blood. It wouldn't be much blood. One drop of blood could easily fill at least fifty of such containers. Yet in the amount of blood in that small container there would be about 5 million red cells. This number was worked out in 1852 by a German scientist, Karl Vierordt (FEER-ort, 1818–1884).

Blood isn't always red, however. It is only red after it returns from the lungs, where it has picked up air. It is the red blood that is pumped out by the left ventricle all over the body. In the body the air is used up, and the blood turns a dark bluish color. It returns to the heart that way and is sent out to the lungs where it turns red again.

This was first pointed out in 1669 by an English doctor, Richard Lower (1631–1691). The blood in the arteries (all except those going to the lungs) is bright red and is called "arterial blood" (ahr-TEE-ree-ul). The blood in the veins (all except those coming from

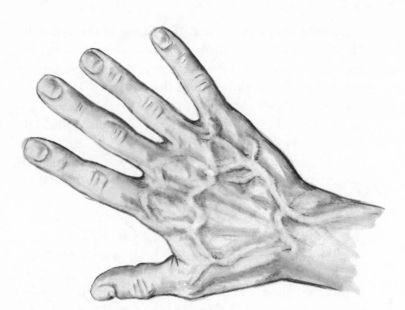

Veins in hand

the lungs) have the dark color and is called "venous blood" (VEE-nus).

If you happen to have fair skin, then look at the back of your hands. You will see veins just under the skin carrying venous blood back to your heart. They look like bluish lines against the skin. They are carrying blood, but it isn't red blood.

Naturally, you can't see the blue lines of the veins if you are dark-skinned, or if you have been out in the sun a good bit and have gotten tanned. In the old days, only well-off people could stay out of the sun. All the poor people had to work in the fields. It was only the wealthy people of Europe, then who had fair, untanned skin and could see the blue veins. That is why they were sometimes called "blue-bloods."

If there were an accident in which a vein was cut, no blue blood would make its appearance. The instant the blood came out of the vein into the air, it would combine with the air and turn red.

What is it in air that turns the blood red?

In 1774, an English chemist, Joseph Priestley (1733–1804) discovered a new gas. In this gas, fires burn very brightly. A piece of wood that is only smoldering will burst into flame if placed in this gas.

In 1778, a French chemist, Antoine Laurent Lavoisier (la-vwah-ZYAY, 1743–1794), was able to show that air consisted of two gases. One fifth of air is Priestley's gas, which Lavoisier called "oxygen" (OK-sih-jen). The other four-fifths is "nitrogen" (NITE-truh-jen).

Oxygen combines with blood and turns it bright red. Arterial blood is "oxygenated."

A German chemist, Julius Lothar Meyer (MY-er, 1830–1895), showed, in 1857, that the oxygen didn't generally mix with the liquid part of the blood. It combines with the red cells.

By that time, it was known that the cells of the body contained complicated substances called "proteins." Each protein was made up of groups of atoms called "molecules" (MOL-uh-kyoolz), and each protein molecule was made up of hundreds, or even thousands, of atoms. In 1851, a German chemist, Otto Funke (FOON-kuh, 1828–1879) had obtained a protein from the red cells. Another German chemist, Ernst Felix Hoppe-Seyler (HOPE-uh-ZY-ler, 1825–1895) purified the protein and studied it carefully.

This red-cell protein is called "hemoglobin" (HEE-moh-GLOH-bin). The "hemo-" is from a Greek word for "blood," and the "-globin" is the name of a kind of protein. Therefore, hemoglobin is "blood protein."

When blood passes through the lungs, the oxygen in the air combines with the dark-colored hemoglobin to form the bright red "oxyhemoglobin" (OK-see-HEE-moh-GLOH-bin). The oxygen is held rather loosely so that, when the blood gets into the capillaries and circulates among all the body cells, the cells can take the oxygen away from the oxyhemoglobin, which becomes just hemoglobin again.

The cells use the oxygen to combine with molecules they obtain from food. In this way, energy is produced, and the body can move and do its work.

In 1747, an Italian chemist, Vincenzo Antonio Menghini (men-Gee-nee, 1704–1759), found that there was a small quantity of iron in blood. It seemed to him that the iron was present in the red cells. Eventually, it was found that every molecule of hemoglobin contained four iron atoms. It was actually to the iron atoms that oxygen atoms attached themselves.

If a person bleeds, he loses some of the iron. Then, if there isn't enough iron in his food, he continues to have a shortage and he suffers from "anemia" (uh-NEE-mee-uh). His blood can't pick up enough oxygen, so that the body is short of energy. A person with anemia tends to be tired all the time.

What if a person bled a great deal and was short of blood? Could some blood be taken from an animal and injected (or "transfused") into the person?

This was tried in the 1600s, and blood was transfused from one animal to another. Richard Lower was the first, in 1666, to try to transfuse blood from an animal into a human being.

Sometimes such transfusion seemed to help, but sometimes it didn't. Occasionally, people died after such a transfusion, so doctors didn't like to try it very often.

An English doctor, James Blundell (1790–1877), finally decided that the blood of a particular kind of animal would only help that particular kind. Therefore, if a human being needed blood it would have to come from another human being. Beginning in 1818, he transfused blood from healthy human beings to other human beings who needed blood.

Again, that sometimes worked and sometimes didn't. When it didn't work, that seemed to be because the red cells in the blood being transfused stuck together tightly, or "agglutinated," when it entered the blood vessels of the patient. The patient, getting clumps of red cells that wouldn't separate and do their work, was worse off than before and might even die.

In 1900, an Austrian doctor, Karl Landsteiner (LAHND-shty-ner, 1868–1943), found the answer. He discovered that there were four kinds of red cells. Some people had a chemical called "A" attached to their red cells, and some had another chemical called "B." For this reason we can talk of "A-type" blood and "B-type" blood. People who had both chemicals attached to their red cells had "AB-type" blood and others, who had neither chemical, had "O-type" blood.

One type of blood will often agglutinate if transfused into a patient with another blood type. It is best, therefore, for a patient to get transfusions of his own blood type. In an emergency, an AB-type patient can accept blood of any other type, but the AB-type is the least common. Only one American in twenty-five is AB-type.

An A-type, or B-type, patient can accept O-type blood fairly well. That is why, when blood is collected for an emergency, O-type blood is particularly useful. It can be given to anyone without too much danger. However, a patient with O-type blood can accept only O-type blood. Fortunately, O-type blood is the most common. Nearly half of all Americans are O-type. In 1930, Landsteiner received a Nobel prize for his work on these blood types.

Some people, by the way, do not like to call red cells by that name.

In 1831, a Scottish scientist, Robert Brown (1773–1858), discovered that there is a little structure in the interior of a cell, and he called that structure a "nucleus" (NYOO-klee-us). It was later learned that every true cell has a nucleus. What's more, the nucleus is the most important part of the cell. It has the substances that make it possible for cells to divide and to make two cells where there once was only one. Cells cannot grow and multiply without a nucleus.

The red cell in human beings (and in many other animals) does *not* have a nucleus and therefore is not a true cell. For that reason, it is sometimes called a "red corpuscle" (KAWR-pus-l).

Red cells, or red corpuscles (whichever you wish to call them), do not live long—perhaps because they don't have a nucleus. Then, too, they work hard, moving about the body, picking up oxygen in the lungs and giving it up to the body, over and over again. After about 125 days, they begin to break up. They're picked up in a part of the body called the

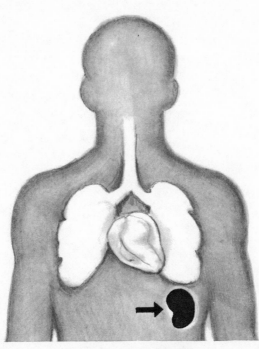

Location of spleen

"spleen" and are eliminated with the body wastes. Only the iron atoms are saved for use in other red cells.

In the body, there are more than 2 million red cells breaking down every second. Altogether, there are so many red cells however, that 2 million isn't a lot. Besides, new red cells are continually being formed in the bone marrow at the same speed with which they break down. The new red cells are formed from parent cells that *do* have a nucleus.

4
The White Cells and Platelets

ALTHOUGH THE RED cells are by far the most numerous objects that float in the blood stream, they are not the only ones.

In 1850, a French doctor, Joseph Casimir Davaine (dah-VAN, 1812-1882), noticed cells in the blood that were much larger than the red cells. They were pale in color and uneven in shape. The ones that Davaine saw moved with "amoeboid motion" (uh-MEE-boid). That is, their motion resembled a common one-celled creature called an "amoeba" (uh-MEE-buh), which is often seen in pond water if one uses a microscope. An amoeba simply thrusts out a bulge in the direction in which it is traveling. The cell fluid flows into the bulge, then another bulge appears and so on. This is the way in which the pale cells in the blood moved.

In 1869, he reported that these cells would flow around and absorb bits of foreign matter introduced into the blood.

These objects are frequently called "white cells" to distinguish them from the red cells. The white cells contain no hemoglobin, no colored substance of any kind. That is why they are so pale. In addition, they differ from the red cells in being complete. Each white cell has a nucleus, sometimes a large nucleus. In 1855, scientists began to call them "leukocytes" (LYOO-koh-sites), which is Greek for "white cells."

The white cells are few in number compared to the red cells. There is only 1 white cell for every 650 red cells. That is why it took so much longer to notice the white cells. Still, even if the white cells are only 1 in 650, there are many billions of white cells in the blood altogether.

A German doctor, Paul Ehrlich (EHR-likh, 1854-1915), was particularly interested in using the new dyes that chemists were making after 1860. It seemed to him that some of these dyes might combine with substances inside a cell and make them visible by giving them color. Different dyes might react with different substances, and in this way a great deal might be learned about the tiny structures inside the cells. (Without color, the inside of a cell is hard to see. All the parts are transparent and look like shadows against a background of shadows.)

Ehrlich worked with all sorts of dyes on all sorts of

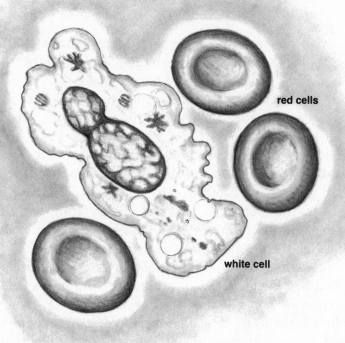

red cells

white cell

Blood cells

cells. About 1875, he used his dyes on white cells, and he found that not all white cells combine with dyes in the same way. He was able to divide the white cells into several different types. Nowadays, five types are well-known and, under normal conditions, always exist in certain proportions to each other. If one or more of them are out of proportion, doctors are warned of the possible presence of disease.

Sometimes, the cells in the bone marrow that make white cells start making many more than are needed. The number of white cells in the blood can get up to 150 times as many as normal. Other cells in the blood are crowded, and the blood no longer does its work well. This condition is known as "leukemia" (lyoo-KEE-mee-uh) and is a very serious disease.

A Russian scientist, Ilya Ilich Mechnikov (MECH-nih-koff, 1845–1916), was particularly interested in "bacteria" (bak-TEE-ree-uh), which are very small one-celled creatures, much smaller than amoebas, and even considerably smaller than red cells. In the 1860s, the French chemist, Louis Pasteur (1822–1895), had shown that bacteria could get into the body and multiply there, causing many common diseases.

But there are bacteria everywhere about us; in the air, in the water, in the soil. Every time we cut ourselves, bacteria are bound to get into the body through the cut. Why don't we all die of disease?

Mechnikov studied the situation carefully. He noticed that whenever there was a cut, white cells were carried to it in great number by the blood. So much blood went to the part that it grew red and inflamed, and was painful from all the pressure of the blood on the vessel walls.

The white cells that were brought to the place immediately attacked the bacteria that had invaded the body and produced an "infection." Usually, the white cells destroy the bacteria and prevent the infection from getting worse.

The white cells of the body thus act as the first line of defense against infection. They are like soldiers who are ready to battle the enemy at any time. They do their work anywhere in the body where bacteria have gained entry, and they are found in the blood because they must be ready to be carried rapidly to any threatened point.

Mechnikov called these bacteria-eating white cells "phagocytes" (FAG-ho-sites), from a Greek word meaning "eating cells." White cells also get rid of

White cells destroying bacteria by engulfing them

unneeded parts of the body. For instance, certain large white cells absorb those red cells that are old and breaking up.

Ehrlich and Mechnikov, because of their work on white cells and in other areas of medicine, shared a Nobel prize in 1908.

When a balloon or an automobile tire is punctured, all the air escapes. When a hot-water bottle is punctured, all the water runs out. When the body is punctured, however, the blood begins to run out, but doesn't continue to do so. Unless the body is very badly mangled, the blood flow stops after awhile and a "clot" forms.

The clot forms in this way. . . .

A protein called "fibrinogen" (fy-BRIN-oh-jen) is dissolved in the blood. When blood is exposed to air, such as when you cut yourself and begin to bleed, the fibrinogen undergoes a small shift of its atoms that changes it into "fibrin" (FY-brin). Fibrin doesn't stay in solution, but comes out of the blood in long threads, which entangle the red cells. It gradually forms a dry crust that covers the opening and stops the bleeding until the skin heals.

Naturally, when scientists began to study this "blood-clotting," they wondered what made the clot form only during bleeding. Why didn't it form in the blood while it was being pushed through the blood vessels?

(Actually, this does happen sometimes, but only very rarely. A clot can form in the bloodstream, and it may then get jammed into a small blood vessel and prevent blood from passing through. This can cause a heart attack or a stroke and may kill. However, the clotting machinery works fairly well and hardly ever goes wrong, so most people don't have to worry about it, especially when they're young and all the body machinery is still new.)

The beginning of an explanation of clotting came in 1842, when a French scientist, Alfred Donné (doh-NAY, 1801–1878), reported a new type of object floating in the bloodstream.

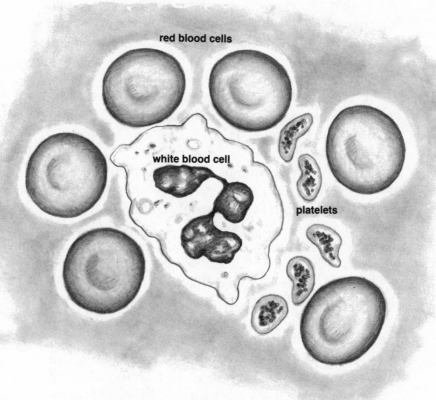

Cells and Platelets in the blood

An Italian doctor, Giulio Csare Bizzozero (BITS-tso-TSEH-roh), studied the new type of object in 1882 and showed that it occurred in blood normally. What's more, it had some connection with clotting. He called the objects "platelets" because their shapes resemble tiny plates. (They actually resemble two plates, placed face to face.) They are also called "thrombocytes" (THROM-boh-sites), which is Greek for "clotting cells."

Platelets are even smaller than red cells. It would take two platelets, side by side, to stretch across a red cell, and it would take eight of them to weigh as much as a red cell.

Platelets are more numerous than white cells. There are about thirty-five platelets for every white cell in the blood. On the other hand, they are not as numerous as red cells. There is only one platelet for every twenty red cells.

Platelets aren't real cells, any more than red cells are. They have no nuclei, and they are even more fragile than red cells are. They only last nine days or so before they break down and have to be swept up and disposed of. Naturally, new ones are constantly being formed.

Platelets manage to keep themselves intact while they are in the bloodstream, but the instant there is a break and bleeding starts, the platelets are exposed to the air and break down.

They release a substance into the blood as a result of the breakdown. The substance starts a long chain of chemical changes that ends with the change of fibrinogen to fibrin and the formation of a clot.

You might wonder why a long chain of chemical

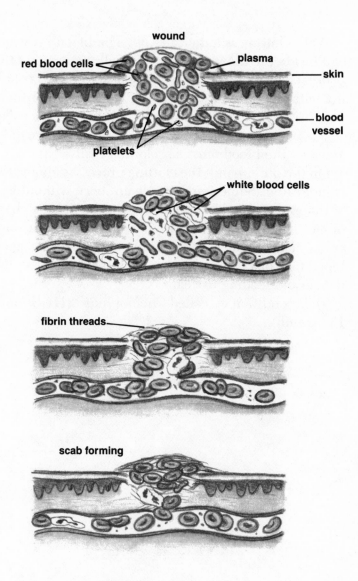

Formation of blood clot

changes is needed. Why shouldn't there just be one change—fibrinogen to fibrin—and, behold, a clot.

47

Well, clotting is a delicate job. The blood must not clot inside the blood vessels. With all the banging the platelets get as they move from place to place, colliding with red cells and the vessel walls, some of them may break. If so, the body must rely on the fact that *some* of the changes can't take place inside the vessels. You see, the blood *must not* clot too easily.

On the other hand, the clotting process is almost *too* complicated. Sometimes people are born without one of the numerous chemicals that form part of the chain of clotting. In that case, their blood clots with difficulty, or not at all. Even a small cut that starts oozing blood may just keep on oozing, and there is always the danger of bleeding to death.

This condition is called "hemophilia" (HEE-moh-FIL-ee-uh).

5
The Plasma

THE RED CELLS, white cells, and platelets make up the "formed elements" of the blood. They are objects that have a form, or shape.

Suppose all the formed elements are removed from the blood. One way of doing it is to whirl a container of blood round and round. When you whirl something, it is forced away from the center. Suppose you have a ball attached to a rubber string, and you whirl it faster and faster. The ball moves away from your hand stretching the string more and more and finally breaking it.

In the container of blood, the formed elements are forced against the bottom of the container as it whirls. Eventually, the formed elements are caked down hard and you can pour the watery part of the blood out of the container.

The formed elements make up about 45 percent, or just under half, of the blood. The watery part makes up about 55 percent. The watery part is called "plasma" (PLAZ-muh), from a Greek word for something that doesn't have any particular form.

The plasma is what makes the blood act as a liquid. If the formed elements were present in the blood vessels all by themselves, the heart wouldn't be able to move them. It's the plasma that moves and carries the formed elements along with itself. The plasma carries the red cells to the lungs to take up oxygen, and then to all the rest of the body to deliver the oxygen. It carries the white cells to any part of the body where they are needed to fight bacteria. It carries the platelets to any part of the body where blood loss must be stopped.

Then, too, the plasma helps even out some of the properties of the body. For instance, the liver has so many chemical changes going on inside its cells that it produces a lot of heat. If the heat just stayed where it was, the liver cells would become too hot and would die. The skin cells, on the other hand, lose heat to the outside and, if they continued to do so, they would get too cold and would die.

The plasma picks up heat at the liver, so that the liver stays cool. The plasma then delivers heat to the skin, so it stays warm. In this way the blood plasma helps even out the temperature in the body to a comfortable figure that doesn't change as long as we remain healthy.

When it is hot outside the little vessels in the skin expand so that there is room for more blood. Extra heat is brought to the skin to be lost there so that we remain cool. When it is cold, the little vessels in the skin contract so that there is less blood there, and the body doesn't lose too much heat. That is why our skin is flushed in hot weather and turns bluish in cold weather.

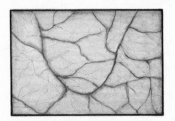 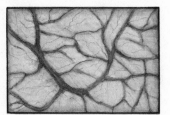

blood vessels in skin constricted   **blood vessels dilated**

Temperature control

Plasma, even if it were nothing but water, could even out heat. However, plasma is only 92 percent water. The other 8 percent consists of substances of one sort or another that are dissolved. These dissolved substances are also important in keeping conditions in the body even and pleasant.

For instance, some chemical changes in the body tend to produce "acids," and some tend to produce "bases" (the opposite of acids). It would kill the cells if the surroundings grew too acidic or too basic. The cells are most comfortable when the surroundings are not too much one way or the other, but are "neutral."

The plasma contains chemicals that tend to combine with acids or with bases. In this way they help keep the surroundings neutral.

The chemicals in plasma also control the way in which water and other substances leak into and out of the tiny blood vessels. The presence of the chemicals sees to it that the right substances leak in and out and that not too much water moves in either direction.

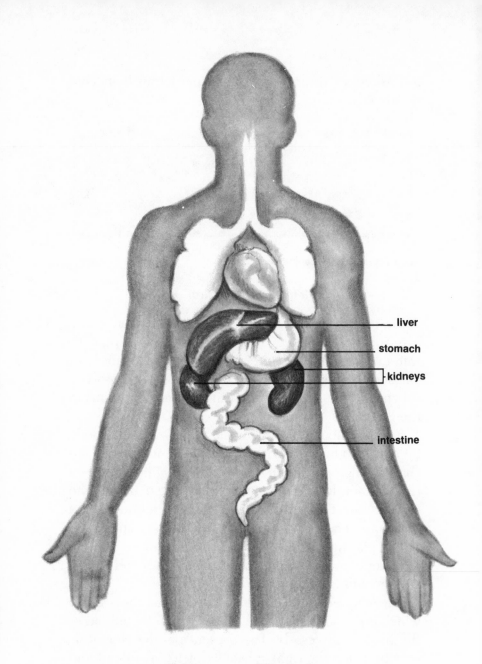

liver

stomach

kidneys

intestine

Major organs of the body

The plasma brings to the body those substances it needs. The oxygen brought by the red cells is not enough. The body also needs materials with which the oxygen can combine to produce energy. These materials come from our food.

The food we eat is digested in the stomach and intestines. Complicated molecules in the food are broken down to smaller molecules that are absorbed through the intestinal wall and enter the plasma. The simple molecules may then be put together into more complicated form and stored in the body as starch or fat for future use. Other simple molecules are built up to form molecules that the body needs, such as protein.

Some simple molecules, however, are kept circulating in the plasma for the body's immediate use. One of these, for instance, is a small sugar molecule called "glucose" (GLOO-kose). Glucose was first detected in blood in 1844, by a German chemist, Carl Schmidt.

The cells of the body absorb glucose from the plasma and combine it with oxygen to produce energy. The brain cells, in particular, use only glucose for this purpose, nothing else. The plasma also carries fatty acids for combination with oxygen. Fatty acids produce more energy than glucose does and are used by muscles, particularly.

Thus, the red cells carry oxygen, and the plasma carries glucose and fatty acids. In this way, the body is supplied with the energy it needs. As the plasma gives up its glucose and fatty acids, more is obtained from food, or from the stores of fat and starch in the body. If we don't get enough food, we lose weight as the fat and starch stores diminish. If we get too much food, the fat supply increases and we gain weight and grow stout.

The body also produces wastes. When oxygen combines with glucose and fatty acids, one of the substances produced is "carbon dioxide" (KAHR-bon dy-OK-side). The carbon dioxide is of no use to the body and, if it just accumulated, it would make the body too acidic and would kill it.

Fortunately, the carbon dioxide dissolves in the plasma. When the blood passes through the lungs and the red cells pick up oxygen, the plasma gives up its carbon dioxide. The air you breathe in is 80 percent nitrogen and 20 percent oxygen, but the air you breathe out is 80 percent nitrogen, 16 percent oxygen, and 4 percent carbon dioxide.

Then, too, when particular protein molecules are no longer needed in the body, they are broken down to small molecules of "urea" (yoo-REE-uh). This was shown in 1842 by a Russian chemist, Friedrich Heinrich Bidder (1810–1894).

The urea would kill the body if it just stayed there, but it too dissolves in the plasma. It is carried to the kidneys, where it is filtered out and is disposed of in the urine.

In other words, the plasma not only brings needed materials to the body cells, it also gets rid of the wastes.

Then, too, some parts of the body produce "hormones" (HAWR-monez). There were first discovered in 1902 by two English scientists, William Maddock Bayliss (1860–1924) and Ernest Henry Starling (1866–1927). These hormones, in small quantities, control many of the body's activities. They enter the plasma

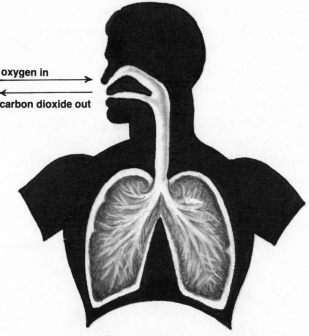

oxygen in →

← carbon dioxide out

Gas exchange

and are carried to any part of the body where they are needed.

For instance, one hormone, "insulin" (IN-syoo-lin), controls the way in which glucose is absorbed by cells and keeps the quantity in the plasma at the proper level. When insulin isn't properly produced, the result is a serious disease called "diabetes" (dy-uh-BEE-teez), in which the plasma level of glucose gets too high.

Nowadays, whenever a person gets a complete medical examination, a sample of blood is always taken. It is analyzed to make sure that the various substances present, the different formed elements and the material dissolved in the plasma are all present in proper amounts. Too much glucose might mean diabetes, for instance. Too much of a fatty substance called "cholesterol" (koh-LES-tuh-rol) may mean a danger of heart attacks, and so on.

More than half the weight of substances dissolved in plasma are proteins. One of these is fibrinogen. It can be kept in the plasma by adding a bit of chemical that will keep it from turning to fibrin. Or else, it can be allowed to turn into fibrin and can then be removed. Plasma without the fibrinogen is called "serum" (SEE-rum).

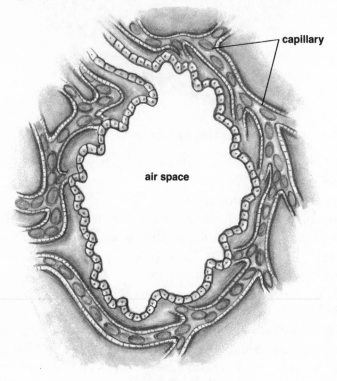

capillary

air space

Lung air sac

The rest of the proteins come in a wide variety of types that are very similar chemically. Fortunately, a Swedish chemist, Arne Wilhelm Tiselius (tih-SAY-lee-us), devised a method called "electrophoresis" (ee-LEK-tro-fur-REE-sis), in 1937 that separates similar proteins. Tiselius was awarded a Nobel Prize for this in 1948.

The proteins fall into two groups: "albumins" (AL-byoo-minz) and "globulins" (GLOB-you-linz). The latter can be further divided into "alpha-globulins" (AL-fuh), "beta-globulins" (BAY-tuh), and "gamma-globulins" (GAM-uh). Alpha, beta, and gamma are the first three letters of the Greek alphabet.

Some of these proteins combine easily with substances the body needs in small amounts—with certain fatty substances, or iron atoms, or copper atoms—and carry these to wherever they are needed.

The gamma-globulins have the capacity to combine with foreign molecules that get into the body—with "viruses," or with poisonous "toxins" produced by bacteria, or with other damaging substances. By combining with them, the gamma-globulins neutralize them. The gamma-globulins that act this way are called "antibodies."

The body keeps a supply of some antibodies that have proved useful. For instance, when you get chicken pox, measles, or mumps, the body manufactures antibodies to fight the annoying germs and to help you recover. After that the antibodies stay, and you don't catch these diseases a second time. You have become "immune" (ih-MYOON).

The gamma-globulins are thus an important part of

the body's "immune mechanism" that protects us from disease.

As you see, then, blood is useful in so many different ways that we can hardly blame the ancients who thought blood was life itself. It almost is.

Index